# TINY PIGGY GOES TO SCHOOL

WRITTEN AND ILLUSTRATED BY
STACEY MOLLUS

Copyright © 2021 by Stacey Mollus
All rights reserved.
ISBN: 978-0-9988713-5-6

This book is dedicated to my amazingly wonderful granddaughter. Rylan bravely started kindergarten this year.

*Rylan, Mimi thinks you are awesome! You are so silly, and you make me laugh all the time. You sing the best songs and come up with the most exciting ideas when we are making up imaginary stories.*

*I am so happy that you share Tiny Piggy with all of us, and even more happy that she is your best friend and not Sodia.*

*I love you!!*

Tiny Piggy was worn out. She had been up very late last night listening to her human, Rylan, talk about the scary place she was going to tomorrow called 'school'.

Rylan told Tiny,

"What if I get confused and sit at the wrong desk? That would be so embarrassing!"

"What if I don't know where the lunchroom is and don't get to eat? What if my stomach growls all afternoon?"

"What if my parents forget to pick me up and I have to sleep at school?"

She held Tiny tightly and said with a sad voice, "What if I get there and no one likes me?"
Tiny Piggy thought, "*School sounds totally awful!*"
Then Rylan told Tiny the scariest thing of all. "I know what will make things better. I will take you with me!"

Those words kept Tiny awake all night.

Now the morning was here, and there was no more thinking about it. It was really happening.

Rylan tucked Tiny into the outside pocket of her backpack, then threw it over her shoulder.

"I am so glad she decided to take me with her," Tiny thought, "but I am kind of scared. I know I can always make her smile if things get too bad, but oh my goodness...I am really heading to school."

Rylan took her mother by the hand and walked out the door.

Tiny stuck her head out of the dark pocket. The sunshine felt good on her face. It made her so happy she almost forgot where they were headed.

Arriving at the building, people were everywhere. Parents, students, and teachers all going in different directions. Rylan looked up at her mommy, hugged her, then bravely said, "I will see you after school."

Tiny Piggy wanted to cry but quickly reminded herself, *"If Rylan can do this, I can too."*

Walking through the front door, there was so much noise. Kids were talking about missing each other over the summer; teachers explaining where classrooms were located; clapping as some of the kids gave each other high-fives. She also heard a lot of laughter. "*Well, this doesn't seem totally awful,*" Tiny Piggy thought.

Tiny held on tightly as Rylan hurried down a long hallway, stopped for a moment, then took a deep breath and walked into her classroom.

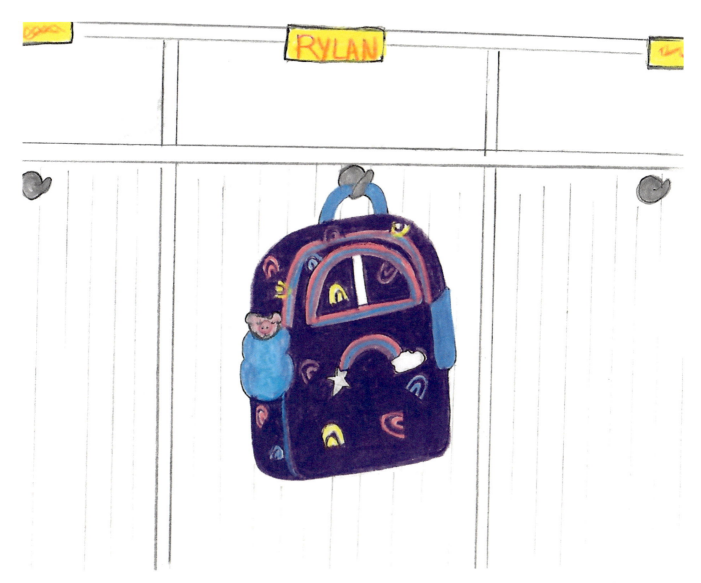

Rylan hung her backpack on a peg, then patted Tiny Piggy on the head and whispered, "I will see you soon."
Tiny peaked over the top of the pocket and watched Rylan take a seat at her desk. She listened closely as the teacher began to speak.

"Hello, class. I am so excited that I get to be your teacher this year. We are going to have such a great time. First, I would like to get to know all of you. Let's introduce ourselves. I will start. I am Mrs. Ross. And you are?" Tiny listened as each child said their name. Some spoke loudly. Some softly.

Tiny got so happy when she heard Rylan introduce herself. *"That's my girl. She sounded okay, not scared at all."*

Relieved that Rylan seemed to be doing well, Tiny tucked herself back into the pocket, stretched out long, and began to relax. Minutes later, she was snoring the softest, sweetest, little piggy snore.

A loud voice shouted, "It's time for recess!" The sound scared the sleeping piggy so badly she almost jumped out of the backpack.

She put her piggy hand on her heart to calm down and let out a long breath. *"Recess? What in the world is recess?"* she thought. She pressed her ear to the pocket, hoping to find out what was about to happen.

Mrs. Ross continued, "You may take any of the toys or sports equipment out to the playground, but make sure you bring them back in when you return to class."

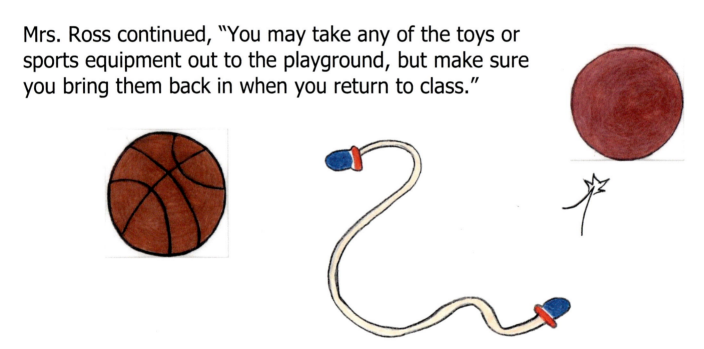

Tiny heard lots of running footsteps. Some of those steps got louder as they were getting closer to her.

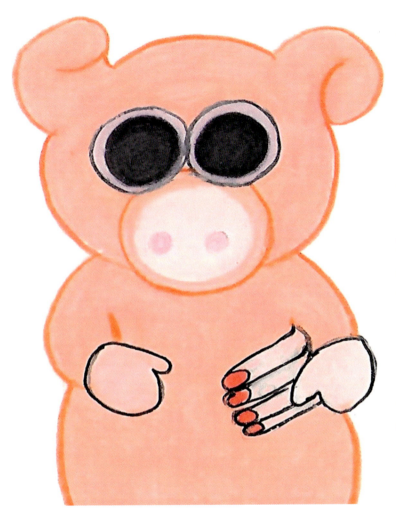

She scrunched up and laid very still so as not to be noticed, when suddenly, a hand reached into the pocket and lifted her out into the light.

It was Rylan's hand.

She gave her piggy a gigantic hug that made them both feel warm inside.

Rylan held Tiny into the air in front of two other little girls about the same size.

"This is my favorite stuffed animal in the whole wide world. We call her Tiny Piggy. She has gone everywhere with me, and she is tons of fun."

One of the other little girls reached up, took Tiny into her hands, and squealed. "Oh, my goodness! She is adorable. I have a great idea. Let's make her some accessories. We can make some sunglasses, and maybe even a crown. I will go grab my construction paper and scissors."

Rylan shouted, "Yes! I love that idea."

Recess was the best! Tiny loved every minute of it and wished it never ended. Not only did the little girls make her some fabulous new items to wear, but they took turns pushing her on the swings and taking her down the slide.

The most exciting part was when one of the boys in Rylan's class grabbed Tiny and ran all over the playground yelling, "You can't catch us!"

Rylan and the two other girls jumped up and down, trying hard to rescue piggy, but Tiny was held up so high in the air that no one even got close.

It was so much fun!

The sound of the teacher's whistle stopped all of the kids in their tracks. The little boy handed Tiny back to Rylan as all the students got into a perfectly straight line and waited for the teacher to open the door.

Rylan looked at Tiny and said, "Shhh," then gently shoved her piggy into her jean jacket as they walked down the hallway.

Tiny did not want to get into any trouble, so she did exactly what she was told.

Once they arrived in the classroom, Rylan opened her jacket and gently placed her piggy deep into the cubby under her desk. She gave a thumbs-up before pulling her hand out of the space. Tiny smiled, happy she had been moved from the closet to a location closer to her friend.

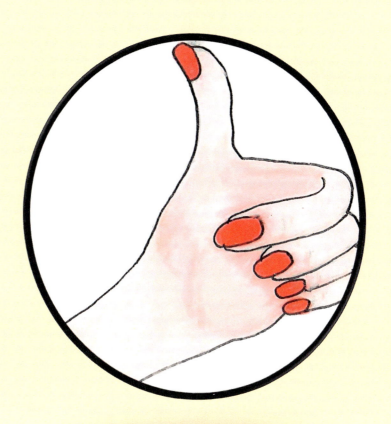

Mrs. Ross said, "It is time for art. Today, we are going to draw something from nature. Please get out your crayons."

Rylan's hand reached into her desk and picked up the box of colors. Tiny laid back on a notebook and dreamed about what kind of picture her friend could be creating. *"I bet she is going to make something fabulous!"*

In a very short time, Rylan finished her drawing, signed her name, then walked up to the desk and handed the colorful picture to her teacher.

Mrs. Ross looked it over and smiled, "Wow, Rylan! That is beautiful. You are quite the little artist."

Tiny was so proud of her person. *"I always knew Rylan was amazing. I am so happy to hear her teacher feels the same way."*

Shortly after the pictures were drawn, Mrs. Ross said, "It is time to eat. Let's put away our art supplies and line up at the door. We will all walk to the lunchroom together."

Tiny got so excited! "Lunchroom? A whole room just for eating? I'm so excited I can hardly sit still!"

Rylan waited until everyone turned around before reaching into her desk and grabbing Tiny. She tucked her back into her jacket, then stepped into line.

Tiny held on tightly as they walked down the long hallway. Once they arrived, she took a long sniff and smiled.
 "Ahhh, the lunchroom is the best smelling room in the whole world!"

The sounds of lunchboxes unzipping; forks scraping across plates; cupcake packages being torn open made the room seem very loud. Everyone seemed to be having a great time.

Tiny thought, *"I wonder what Rylan brought in her lunch today?"*
She could hear the sandwich being unwrapped. She took another big sniff to see if she could tell if it was peanut butter and jelly or a turkey and cheese sandwich with mustard (two of Rylan's favorite things to eat). Tiny licked her lips at the thought.

Rylan lifted the bread, removed the cheese, and tossed it on the table by her milk carton.
"I need to let my mommy know that I don't like cheese on my sandwich," she said before taking a big bite.

Tiny listened from the jacket pocket as one of the girls who played with Rylan at recess offered to share her cheese and crackers.

Tiny smiled because she knew sharing meant Rylan had a new friend.

Lunch went by pretty quickly, and after the children were seated back at their desks, it got very quiet.
A book was read and instructions were given. Then Mrs. Ross said, "It is time to put everything away and get ready to go home. It was a great first day. I am so excited that you are in my class, and I'm looking forward to seeing you again tomorrow."

Rylan put all of her papers and notes in her backpack, squeezed Tiny deeply into the side pocket, and headed out the door when the bell rang.

Tiny could tell Rylan got very excited when she saw her parents standing at the end of the drive because she took off skipping down the sidewalk. Tiny held on with all of her might as the backpack bounced around. The second she got close her daddy got down on his knee. She threw her arms around his neck and hugged him tightly. "How was your first day?" he asked. "I had the best time!" Rylan said.

Rylan climbed into bed that night and gave Tiny an extra big squeeze before tucking her under the blankets. "Wasn't today fun? School is so awesome. Thank you so much for being there with me today." she said. "I love you so much, Tiny Piggy. You are my best friend." She snuggled Tiny as she nodded off to sleep.

As Tiny lay there, a smile crossed her pink face. *"I was so scared about going to school, but I was scared for nothing. School is a huge building, but everyone was so nice. I met a ton of new friends, learned fun stuff, and that lunchroom smells delicious!"* Tiny cuddled in closer to her person. *"I hope she takes me to school EVERY day."*

Hello. My name is Stacey Mollus, and I love to ride around with Rylan, giving Jeep waves. I also love to write books. As a matter of fact, I wrote the one that you just read. I sure hope it made you smile, because it made my heart very happy to write it. If you enjoyed it, feel free to purchase the others in my series called "Mimi's Loves". There are six books in the collection, one for each of my adorably squishy grandchildren.
You can find my books on Amazon or send me a note at **staceymollus@gmail.com**.

Keep reading! It makes your brain happy.

**Bonus nugget of goodness**: As you can see from these photos, there is a real-life Tiny Piggy, and she really went to school with Rylan on her first day. They had a fabulous time!

Made in the USA
Coppell, TX
23 February 2022

73985175R00024